Listen to the Children

Listen to the Children

Stories collected by
Docia Zavitkovsky

Commentaries by
Katherine Read Baker

Photographs by
Jean Reiss Berlfein

Introduction and Questions to
consider by
Millie Almy

Created and produced by
Jean Reiss Berlfein

National Association for the
Education of Young Children
Washington, D.C.

The National Association for the Education of Young Children (NAEYC) attempts through its publications program to provide a forum for discussion of major issues and ideas in our field. We hope to provoke thought and promote professional growth. The views expressed or implied are not necessarily those of the Association. NAEYC wishes to thank the authors, who donated much time and effort to develop this book as a contribution to our profession.

Photographs © 1986 by Jean Reiss Berlfein.

National Association for the Education of Young Children
1509 16th Street, N.W.
Washington, DC 20036–1426

Library of Congress Catalog Card Number: 86-60493

ISBN Catalog Number: 0-935989-00-5

NAEYC #304

Printed in the United States of America.

Introduction

Listen to the Children is a book to enjoy. Jean Berlfein's photographs capture some wonderful moments in the lives of children from the ages of 2 through 5. As you look at her photos, try to figure out what is going on, then turn to the stories the photographs illustrate.

Docia Zavitkovsky's stories were collected during the 40 years she taught preschoolers, directed child care centers, shared with parents, and worked with teachers and teachers-to-be. There is a chuckle in many of the stories, a touch of pathos in others. Some of the situations may stir up memories of your own childhood, reminding you of the child that lives on in each of us. If you have children, or have taught young children, you probably will recall favorite anecdotes from your own experiences.

Why do early childhood teachers enjoy stories such as these? Often we remember an anecdote because we find a child's way of looking at the world fresh and amusing. When we know the child and reflect on what she or he has said or done, we often find new meaning in it. Certain incidents reveal thoughts and feelings that help adults understand better what it is like to be a child—that particular child or any child.

Some of the stories also reflect how adults relate to children—our artistry or our ineptitude. Teachers will appreciate these observations because they illustrate so concretely the principles that are part of our profession's knowledge base.

After you have looked at the photographs and read the stories, you are ready to turn to the commentaries by Katherine Read Baker, to see what the stories mean to her. She draws on her knowledge of child development and learning and on many years of experience in the field. As you reflect on her comments you can move beyond the fun of sharing a child's views to the more intellectual enjoyment that comes from insight into how children feel and learn.

There are also questions to consider with each section. Some may lead you to read more about child development. Others may stimulate your thinking about the complex context of social and economic realities, and of the diverse values in which today's parents and teachers make decisions that affect children.

Our intent in producing this book is that individual readers will enjoy and learn from our experiences. However, *Listen to the Children* is also a book to share with others—staff or parents in a program for young children, or a class in early childhood education. Each photo and story is likely to stimulate many differing points of view. Open examination and exploration of these differences is an essential step in reaching shared meanings and understanding. Agreement of this kind underlies the resolution of common problems that arise when teachers and parents work together.

Millie Almy
February 1986

Introduction

Listen to the Children . . .

. . . When They Trust an Adult to Understand

. . . When They Develop Self-Control

. . . When They Figure Things Out

. . . When They Interact With Others

And Listen to Parents When . . .

Acknowledgments

Information About NAEYC

About the Authors

... When They Trust an Adult to Understand

"My feet might think I'm falling"

Peggy has been standing on top of the jumping board for quite a while. When the teacher walks over to her, Peggy says, "I want to jump off, but my feet might think I'm falling."

The teacher suggests she tell her feet she is jumping. Peggy bends down, looks at her feet, and announces, "I'm jumping." Then she jumps off the board and lands on the ground with a smile.

Commentary

Peggy has a delightful way of putting her feelings into words. She wants to jump, but she is afraid, so she projects her fear onto her feet. Fortunately for her, the teacher responds in an imaginative way with a positive suggestion. Peggy accepts the teacher's suggestion and jumps successfully. She conquers her fear.

Young children are often helped by a playful, imaginative approach when feelings are hard to face. The world of fantasy, a seemingly magic world, is the child's world—wishes and fantasies are important. It takes time for children to sort out the fanciful from the actual and come to grips with reality. Children are fortunate when they are able to face reality without losing touch with the world of magic.

Peggy is aware of her fear, but she makes it manageable when she deals with it through fantasy. She appears to be a child who enjoys stretching her imagination and engaging in creative activities.

Some children in the early primary years still may be unable to distinguish consistently between fantasy and reality, perhaps because they do not trust others. These children need an understanding adult to help them face the real world. For these children a quiet comment, such as, "What do you think *really* happened?" may be enough to help them make a clearer distinction between fantasy and reality.

When we are able to interpret what children really mean, and respond in a way that matches their thinking, we give them an opportunity to cope in a positive way with the world.

Questions to consider

In what other situations might it be helpful for a teacher or parent to assist a child by using fantasy? Under what circumstances is this type of response inadvisable?

"Excuse me" or "Thank you"?

Megin, who has been at the center for less than a week, is just beginning to learn the language, routines, and expectations of her new world. She sits close to the teacher. As she eats, she watches the other children, all of whom are relaxed and comfortable. When she finishes eating her lunch, she turns to the teacher and says, "Thank you."

The teacher replies, "You're welcome."

Megin repeats "Thank you" and the teacher repeats "You're welcome." Megin appears to be uncertain about what to do next. The teacher observes her distress and asks Megin, "What is the matter?"

Megin explains that she wants to go outside to play. She thought "Thank you" was what she was supposed to say when she had finished eating and wanted to leave the table.

Commentary

Megin learns more than simply which words she is expected to use before leaving the table—she also learns that she need not be afraid of making "mistakes" at her center, and that eating is a pleasant experience. The teacher notices her concern right away, finds out what Megin is attempting to communicate, and explains the use of the two phrases. Her teacher is helpful, not critical.

During lunch, Megin intently watches the other children who are eating in a variety of ways. Megin feels comfortable and relaxed. The center is a good place for children to be.

Table manners are important, but they are learned gradually. Eating should be a satisfying experience. Children enjoy exploring as they learn to fit into the patterns adults have established for them. There is no one way that is "right," even within the United States. Many children in child care programs are adjusting to two somewhat different cultures. They need to learn that there is more than one "right" way.

Parents and teachers can all set a good example of the manners acceptable in their cultures. Children will observe and imitate those expectations at home and at school. Soon they are likely to use the behavior acceptable in each culture. Children learn an amazing amount in their own way and at their own pace.

Questions to consider

List some "mistakes" made by young children. In each case, try to figure out what the child may have been thinking. How did the adults assist the child's understanding? Or further confuse it?

4

"You need to put on your sweater"

Jessie is standing at the back fence of the center watching the clouds move swiftly across the sky, the grass wave in the wind, and the palm tree sway from side to side. When her teacher comes out, Jessie exclaims, "Look! Look at the clouds! Look at the grass wiggling. Look at the yellow flowers shaking their faces at each other, and the grass talking back...!"

The teacher replies, "If you're going to stand out here in the cold, you need to put on your sweater."

Commentary

How sad that some teachers are more concerned about sweaters than clouds or waving grass! For Jessie, watching the clouds and the movement of the grasses is a wonderful experience. She expresses her thoughts in imaginative and delightful ways. Jessie seems to feel part of nature. She is eager to share her pleasure, but her teacher is only aware of a girl who should be wearing a sweater on a cold day. What could have limited the teacher's awareness so sadly?

We all know that pressures, of many kinds, sometimes pile up until we fail to be aware of what is really important to children at a significant moment. This teacher may have been busy and harried, but it would have been so easy to take a moment to show appreciation for the loveliness Jessie was seeing, to say a few words, or just to listen with interest. She might then have quietly brought Jessie's sweater to her, so as not to interrupt this significant experience.

Jessie shows unusual sensitivity to beauty and is an imaginative child. Will she continue to feel pleasure in nature and to use her imagination through the years ahead? Will she meet teachers who can perceive and encourage an imaginative and creative child? Or will her attention be channeled into a world of ditto sheets and drills, neatness, and staying in the lines? Will she have teachers who are more concerned with these aspects than with the excitement of watching clouds on a windy day?

Questions to consider

What does this episode tell us about appropriate curriculum activities and teaching methods for young children?

How can harried teachers and parents help each other to recognize, appreciate, and build upon these teachable moments? What can they do to eliminate the stress that often interferes with staying in tune with children?

"Mommy, don't go home"

It was 4-year-old Roberta's second day at the child care center. Her mother, Mrs. Zavala, stayed the first day because she wanted to see the program in action to reassure herself that she had made a good choice. She is staying again because she wants to be sure Roberta feels comfortable before she leaves for work.

After an hour, Roberta has not moved too far from her mother's side. Mrs. Zavala thinks it might be easier for both of them if she tells Roberta that she is just going to step out for a few minutes.

When she tells Roberta, Roberta moves in a little closer so that their bodies touch one another and whispers, "Mommy, don't go home."

Commentary

How does this child feel? How does her mother feel? Both are newcomers, unsure of what to expect or what is expected of them in the group. They are observing.

Mrs. Zavala's curled up toe suggests her uncertainty. Her solution, to try to ease away rather than to honestly face the separation, suggests the situation is difficult for her as well as for Roberta.

Roberta stands close to her mother—the contact must give her a feeling of security. Because she is not holding her mother's hand or watching her face, Roberta seems to have sufficient trust that her mother will not abandon her. Her hands look relaxed, but her smile is rather fixed and tentative. She is watching, and looks interested, but she is not yet ready to participate. She is wearing the tag with her symbol or name, but it does not seem to be part of her.

Mother and daughter are going into a new situation together. They are sharing in an adventure, and they help each other.

Roberta seems to be summoning up her courage to face the new experience. She will feel more confident after she has observed what happens. It will take time and a nurturing mother and teacher before Roberta will be ready to participate.

A child who trusts that her mother will not leave her is able to be more independent and adventurous. When Roberta recognizes that her mother plans to leave for the remainder of the day, her trust in her mother is diminished. Roberta is cautious in this new situation, but she will be ready to explore and discover in time. A parent who is perceptive about and sensitive to a child's needs will be patient and not try to rush the process.

Questions to consider

Separation is a critical issue in child care, and one in which parents and teachers can work closely together to ease the tension for everyone involved. How can center staff help children and parents feel comfortable during the getting acquainted period? How can staff help parents and children deal with the intense feelings of separation? What can parents do to ease the adjustment for themselves and for their children?

How might arrangements for introducing new children differ between programs that admit children throughout the year and those that enroll all children at one time?

Recall other times when an adult failed to be straightforward in dealing with a child. What happened? Why?

"I still love you, Dad"

Tess's parents are busy in the kitchen while Tess is playing in her room with crayons and scissors. When the dishes are done, Dad comes in to read to Tess, only to find she has given herself a haircut—"because my bangs were in my eyes."

Dad is really upset! He shouts, "I still love you, Tess, but I'm very, very angry at what you've done."

An hour or so later, when some of the anger has dissipated, Dad says, "Come, Tess, I'll show you how you look in the bathroom mirror."

Tess looks, turns to her Dad, and says, "It's OK, Dad. I still love you."

Commentary

Tess's father is very angry about what Tess did to her hair, but he adds that he still loves her. Distinguishing between a child's act and the bond of love is not always easy. Tess can feel sure of her father's love even though he makes clear that he disapproves of her behavior.

Later, when her father shows her in the mirror how she looks, she seems to feel the need to forgive his anger toward her with her assurance, "I still love you."

Relationships based firmly on love are worthwhile relationships and a sound basis for discipline. Tess knows how her father feels about her ragged hair, she wants to please him, and she now has a better sense of the proper use of scissors.

How tragic it is for a young child when loss of love is used as a threat: "I won't love you if you. . . ." Such a remark can damage the feeling of trust and security every child needs. Young children are very vulnerable. Their confidence in themselves is easily shaken. They need the support love gives as they learn about acceptable behavior. Feeling sure of being loved is important for healthy personality development in childhood.

Tess is fortunate to have a father who can control his anger. He reassures Tess about his love for her while firmly expressing his disapproval. Tess understands.

Questions to consider

It is not easy for parents or teachers to distinguish between their feelings about a child's behavior and feelings for the child. How can we help children to learn to make this distinction? What do some of us do that can hinder this important learning process?

10

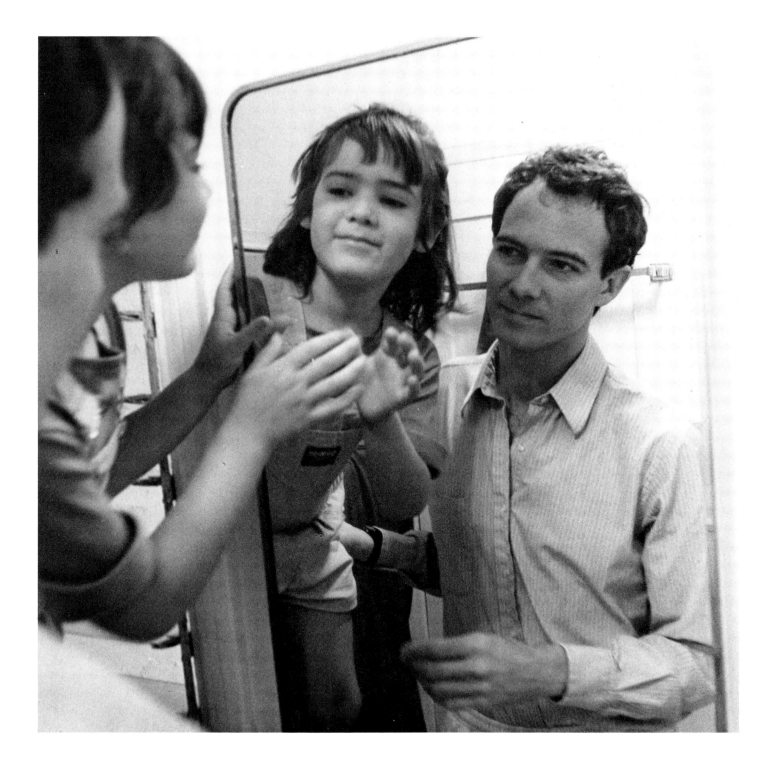

"He should have finded himself a cabbage"

Timmy planted some seeds in the school garden and then asked when they would grow flowers. The teacher, Dot, told him this would happen in the spring, after winter was over, and said "Sometimes it is hard to wait so long, but spring will come."

That winter, Timmy would pause by the birch tree from time to time, peer intently at his planting place, and report to Dot that he couldn't see his flowers . . . when would they grow? Each time the two of them would talk about the seasons and wait for spring.

Finally, one sunny morning, Timmy noticed the cracks in the earth and a few tips of green that barely showed, and he shouted excitedly that his flowers had "growed." The children and Dot hurried over to share the wonder of his discovery. Each day the shoots grew longer and greener, and one day golden buds appeared. Dot told him that on the next day they would probably bloom.

The next morning Timmy arrived earlier than usual and rushed over to see his flowers. They were gone. In their place was a ragged row of chewed-off petals. He ran to Dot and together they looked at the strange sight. As sympathetically as she could, Dot consoled Timmy, saying, "I think the little rabbit who runs into our yard came and nibbled your flowers." They stood quietly together. She took his hand and held it tightly in her own. Timmy looked at the ground. Then, as he gazed directly into her eyes he said gently, "He should have finded himself a cabbage."

Commentary

How fortunate young children would be if all adults were as sensitive and understanding as Dot! Her program offers a wide variety of experiences to children. Timmy is especially interested in growing plants. Dot recognizes this interest and all through the winter, she encourages him to look ahead, "Spring will come." Each time Timmy asks about plants, Dot uses the opportunity to discuss the seasons and the need to wait for growth. When Timmy discovers his first shoots, Dot shares in the excitement of his discovery. She appreciates his sustained interest. Finally, when the tragedy of chewed off buds occurs, Timmy is able to run to his teacher, overwhelmed. He trusts her to understand.

Dot's explanation is given gently, but the facts are stated. They stand together, quietly, and she holds his hand tightly. She is giving him time to absorb the experience, not intruding with words but expressing her sympathy through the tight hand clasp. When Timmy is ready, he can look up straight into his teacher's eyes and give her his wonderful conclusion. It is not an expression of bitterness or anguish, but one of sorrowful understanding, "He should have finded himself a cabbage." For Timmy the experience is now completed.

Dot helps Timmy find his way through the experience and gain strength in facing reality. She demonstrates teaching on the highest level, one that offers hope of peaceful coexistence as people become capable of the kind of communication Dot and Timmy have together.

Questions to consider

What kinds of experiences promote the intellectual and empathetic understanding that Timmy appears to have?

Consider reactions that less sensitive adults might have had. What would they have communicated to Timmy?

12

... When They Develop Self-Control

"Get your wiggles out"

The teacher is showing slides to the children. Between shows, she suggests they get up to jump and stretch to get their wiggles out.

Just as she is about to start the projector again, Christine and three friends come running up to her.

The teacher looks at Christine and asks, "What is it?"

Christine reports, "Ian is bothering us. He didn't get all his wiggles out."

Commentary

This teacher has a delightful way of labeling the process through which young children settle down and become quiet after active play. Getting rid of wiggles on demand is seldom an easy process. Each child has her or his own way and time to achieve quiet.

A group of young children without wiggles would be cause for concern. Such passivity might indicate a lack of interest or stimulation, or it might indicate an authoritarian regime. None of these situations is suitable for productive learning.

A healthy group of children needs a patient teacher, one who is able to accept the various ways in which individual children respond to the request for quiet. The teacher is probably the one who has wiggles if she expects all of the children to succeed in losing their wiggles quickly.

The children who run to report that Ian didn't get all of his wiggles out may be having trouble with their own wiggles. Wiggles don't disappear on demand.

Question to consider

What are the features of appropriate programs for young children that result in the least need for children to get their wiggles out?

"Hit him!"

Kevin and Greg are building together with blocks. Kevin gets angry because Greg takes a block from him. They fight. The teacher intervenes, and talks with Kevin about using words instead of fists. She tells him to try talking to Greg instead of hitting him—to tell Greg what was making him angry. Finally, believing she has made her point, she asks Kevin, "Now, what would you like to do?"

Kevin answers without hesitation, "Hit him!" And he does!

Commentary

This teacher did not get the response she wanted. Why did she fail? Probably because *she* was doing the talking, not the children. Lecturing by the adult is seldom effective as a discipline technique. Neither is punishment.

Four-year-olds feel strongly and they are apt to act speedily. Their impulsiveness often leads them into trouble. They are likely to feel resentment rather than regret as a result of being punished for their behavior. But 4-year-olds are capable of reasoning on their own level, especially when adults have set good examples. Kevin might have given a different response if the teacher had helped him do his own reasoning—to solve the problem himself.

First of all, the teacher needs to establish that hitting is not acceptable behavior and will not be permitted. Then she will be ready to ask, "What is the problem?" She needs to listen carefully to what each child says, perhaps restating a point to make it clear to both children. Then she can ask, "What can we do about it?" or "How can we settle this matter?" Questions like these challenge 4-year-olds to think and reason. The problem is theirs and they need to work out a solution. Many times the solutions children arrive at are creative and acceptable to everyone. Their solutions suit the situation as they see it. The incident thus becomes a problem-solving opportunity.

This process will need to be repeated many times, of course. Other problems will keep cropping up. But given time and patience, children can learn acceptable, constructive patterns for solving problems. These positive approaches set patterns that will last a lifetime.

Questions to consider

What kinds of adult attitudes help children learn to reason effectively? What can adults say to facilitate problem solving? Why do adults sometimes say "I just can't seem to reason with that child"?

"Her's too good to bite him"

A fight develops in the sandbox, and in the midst of the hassle, Betsy bites George. The teacher separates them, talks with the two children, and then walks Betsy to the office to talk with the program director. The two of them talk about biting and anger. Then the director suggests that Betsy go back and talk it over with her teacher, Mrs. Baker. Betsy looks up, a little puzzled. "It wouldn't do any good to tell Mrs. Baker, 'cause her's too good to bite him."

Commentary

What should be done? We see Betsy sitting in the director's office looking puzzled and somewhat disturbed. Betsy is aware that there is a problem with biting, but she is confused about the purpose of talking it over with her teacher, because she is sure her teacher doesn't have a biting problem.

Betsy seems to be a friendly, reasonable child, but she has a primitive and potentially harmful way of defending herself. She needs help to stop biting.

Biting is sometimes what children resort to if they have feelings that are strong and hard to manage. These children feel helpless to control angry feelings. They need help to find other ways to channel their anger. These children often have an abundance of friendly feelings, too. Conflicting feelings are hard for anyone to handle. Betsy is puzzled because she does not believe her teacher has angry feelings.

In this case, an understanding teacher might have stopped the fight before it escalated. If a teacher knows that a child has a biting problem, he can put an arm around the child while suggesting that each child talk about what the trouble seems to be. Children usually have more insight than we give them credit for. This kind of talking, encouraged by a sympathetic teacher, usually drains off much of the anger. Children are then ready to consider other ways to behave.

To help Betsy stop biting, the teacher will need to step quickly into any situation where Betsy might be tempted to resolve it by biting. Prevention is the best solution.

Questions to consider

Why is biting so dangerous?

List and evaluate specific ways to prevent biting.

If biting does occur, what should the teacher do or say to the biter, the bitten, and the parents of both? Should other children be included in the discussion? Why?

18

"Did you have a boy or a girl?"

A regular volunteer at a child care center, who has been in the hospital for a simple operation, was missed by all the children. On her first day back at the center, Rita, a child with a physical handicap, comes over to welcome her back. After exchanging a big hug and a smile, she asks, "Did you have a boy or a girl?"

Commentary

Rita appears to be a friendly, social child. She notices the absence of the volunteer and is quick to welcome her back. Rita also is a child who appears to have had experience with babies being added to families. She knows that a question often asked when people come from the hospital is "Did you have a boy or a girl?"

Rita's question gives the volunteer and/or the teacher an opportunity to talk with Rita and any interested children about older people and some of the reasons they do not have babies. Because of her own limitations, Rita may be more ready than most children to understand about aging and the limitations of older people, as well as about what hospitals do for people.

Four- and 5-year-old children may be aware that older people do not run and climb and play as they do. They may realize that elderly people need a helping hand at times. Elderly people get tired and need to rest frequently, and may forget things. But older people often have more time to listen to children, and they sometimes tell wonderful stories.

Relations between children and older adults can be very satisfying for everyone. Many children enjoy experiences with grandparents, and grandparents are happy to be with grandchildren. Some children may not know their extended family. Older people in the neighborhood are often interested and willing to visit a program for young children regularly; if not, frequent visits can be arranged with a residential care facility for the elderly. Children and adults will benefit from these contacts. Aging is part of the cycle of life for everyone.

Questions to consider

Confusions like Rita's are common among young children. Consider similar instances you have known. Why did children think as they did? What did the adults do to help children gain a better understanding?

Assume that a group of older adults have volunteered to assist in a program for young children. How should the staff, the children, the parents, and the volunteers be prepared?

28

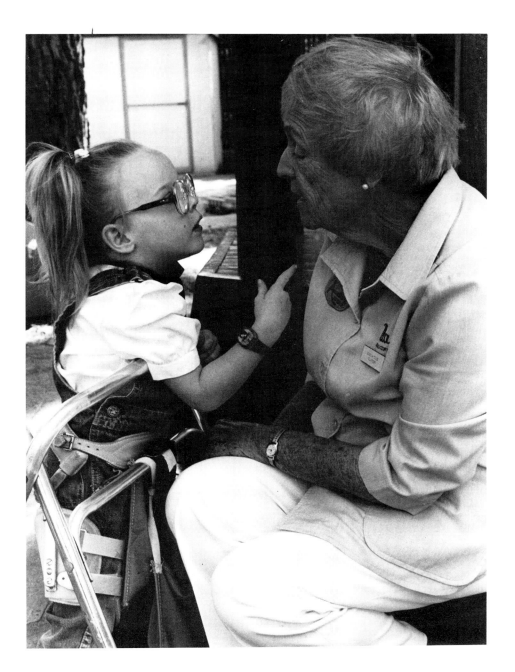

"Do boys ever have babies?"

Three-year-old Ben is large for his age. He talks very little and when he speaks he is deliberate and solemn. He does not participate much in active play, but he observes everything.

A former teacher of his group is visiting with her baby. The children are very interested in the baby and glad to see the mother again. While they are there, the mother nurses her baby. Most of the children are fascinated and ask many questions that the mother answers. Ben is among the children who observe very closely but do not speak. Finally, he summons his courage and asks in a confidential, almost pleading way, "Do boys ever have babies?"

Commentary

Ben seems to have an idea that this is not the case, but he hopes there just might be a chance. Nursing looks like such a desirable experience! His teacher's answer is, "No," but she adds, "Boys can be fathers and take care of their babies."

Ben's question gives the teacher the opportunity to discuss some of the ways boys can expect to have experiences with babies. As fathers they can bathe, dress, feed, change, and play with their babies. Ben may be encouraged to talk about what he and his father do together. Fathers take on many roles with young children, building close relationships. Both boys and girls profit from having a man participate in caring for them.

The teacher may also be able to give children opportunities to observe patterns of caring for young in the animal and human world. Pets like guinea pigs are likely to reproduce. Sometimes birds will bring food to their newly hatched chicks. Both boys and girls enjoy playing with dolls in the housekeeping area.

All children are interested in babies. As they observe babies, human or animal, they ask many questions. They need simple, but truthful, answers. These answers, and children's other experiences with babies, are part of preparation for parenthood in the future.

What a good father Ben may make some day.

Questions to consider

Think about a good program for young children that you know. How many of the staff are female? How many male? What are the reasons for the probable preponderance of females?

List the activities, materials, and equipment available to the children at home or in a program. Classify each item as traditionally masculine, traditionally feminine, or neutral. When the children are free to choose, do they follow tradition or not? Do early childhood programs have a responsibility to provide equal opportunity to both sexes?

How do adults' attitudes about sex and sex roles affect children's thinking?

"You're old enough and big enough"

Susan is playing in the dress-up corner and decides to put curlers in her hair. She asks the teacher to help her. The teacher tries, but cannot make the curler stay in. "I'm sorry, I can't do it," the teacher confesses.

Susan, looking quizzically from the corner of her eye, asks, "Why not? You're old enough and big enough."

Commentary

Susan's question is a reasonable one. Surely a teacher should be able to fix a curler in a child's hair. Susan's reasoning is based on her experience. She probably has been told more than once, "No, you aren't old enough to do that" or "You're not big enough yet." Now she meets a teacher who is old and big and yet she can't fix a curler in a child's hair.

When children are young, they usually feel that adults can do almost anything. It comes as something of a shock to them when they realize that limitations exist even for powerful adults, and that the reasons adults give do not always seem to fit the facts.

Susan's question shows she is doing some thinking and wondering. The teacher has a chance to help Susan think about some of the answers and to extend her understanding about adults and the process of growing up.

The teacher may say, "Yes, I am older than you, and bigger, but I still am finding it hard to fix your curler. I think I need to learn more about curlers."

It is likely that Susan may add, "My Mother knows how." The teacher will acknowledge the mother's accomplishment and together Susan and the teacher may decide to look for someone who does know about curlers. Susan is finding out that everyone keeps on learning, even teachers, and doubting and questioning are part of learning.

Questions to consider

How can adults support children's reasoning and encourage their thoughtful reflection? When might the best policy be to say nothing and give the child time to think?

"Mary had a little . . . lamb"

It is lunch time in a private nursery school. The regular teacher is away. As the children sit down at the table, they tell the substitute they usually say grace before they eat. The teacher, somewhat unsure of her role in this ritual, replies, "You go ahead."

The children fold their hands, bow their heads, and, after a short silence, Stephanie assumes the leadership and begins, "Mary had a little . . . lamb."

Commentary

Neither the teacher nor the children are prepared for this situation. The teacher had not expected that the children would say grace and very wisely asks the children to take the lead. Evidently, however, the teacher is the one who usually says grace. So an enterprising child steps into the breach and speaks up very gravely. Perhaps she likes that poem, or maybe she heard about Mary and a lamb in a church service.

Stephanie has leadership qualities. Her selection for grace indicates her level of understanding of what grace is. The meaning of much that adults do and say is incomprehensible to children, but they strive to make sense of it. Play enables them to re-create situations and rehearse roles in an effort to understand more about the world. Too often we expect children to understand long before they have the experiential background or the maturity of thinking necessary.

Every culture has its own religious beliefs and traditions. Children can share in these observances with family members and begin to establish roots in their own culture. In group settings, children may also have the opportunity to realize there are other cultures with different beliefs and observances. What a marvelous way for them to begin to learn to respect and understand those differences!

Questions to consider

What part should rituals, especially those where children may not yet understand the meaning, have in programs for young children?

What other types of activities can help children learn to appreciate their similarities and differences?

"I just helped a rattler"

Marcia is taking a group of 4-year-olds to the park. Before they go, she tells them there are many toddlers there and they should be careful because toddlers are younger and can be hurt easily. The children have been playing for a while, when Sarah suddenly comes running to Marcia, holding a small child by the hand. Proudly she announces, "I just helped this rattler!"

Commentary

Four-year-olds' vocabularies and social awareness increase rapidly. Sarah gives us an example not only of her confusion of words but also of the satisfaction she feels in caring for someone smaller than she. Concern for and cooperation with others are certainly characteristics to be encouraged.

Sarah is excited and pleased to have the opportunity to help the "rattler." She eagerly shares her pleasure with her teacher, who had encouraged this kind of behavior. From the expression on the face of the younger child, we can see that he enjoys getting attention from a big girl.

When families were large, most children helped care for younger children. We can still provide this experience within the context of groups of children, much like an extended family. Sarah's teacher helps give this experience to her group when she takes them to the park and gives them careful instructions about being considerate of toddlers.

Other opportunities for children to be considerate exist every day—helping a handicapped child if needed, showing a new child around the center, or helping a non-English speaker communicate with others. Being aware of the needs of other people is an important part of social growth in a society that values all of its members. The need for social understanding is greater than ever before.

Question to consider

Assume that a program has as its major goal the promotion of social understanding. What would its curriculum and routines be?

"I just helped her cry"

Kim is waiting at home for her son Billy who is playing next door. When he arrives 20 minutes later than scheduled, she asks what happened.

"Well, Mom," he begins in a grown-up fashion, "Alison's doll broke and I wanted to help her."

"I didn't know you knew how to fix dolls," is his mother's somewhat surprised reaction.

"Oh no, Mom. I *don't* know how. I just stayed to help her cry."

Commentary

Supporting a friend in a good cry is an act of real understanding. Billy knows what Alison needs. These two children have probably been playing together for as long as they can remember. Alison's doll may have been a part of their play on many occasions. When her doll breaks, Billy is there to help. He accepts Alison's need to cry over the doll and gives her his support. He understands that crying is a wonderful release when faced with tragedies, large or small, by boys or girls. Almost anyone with experience can mend a doll, but how many people are able to give support in a good cry?

Billy seems to feel satisfied with himself. He has succeeded as a comforter, and has shown real understanding for Alison. She accepts his comfort. Their friendship is strengthened. Billy is also confident that his mother will understand why he is late returning home. There must be an abundance of trust and consideration in Billy's home.

Questions to consider

How can we help children be sensitive to the feelings of others?

When can children be reassured that it is OK to cry?

When is crying excessive and what should be done about it?

Are there times when children, boys as well as girls, should be encouraged to cry?

"I'll be your Mommy 'til your Mommy comes"

Diana is new at the center, and she is having a difficult time adjusting. Her mother has been gone about half an hour when suddenly Diana begins to cry. Laurie, a 3-year-old passing by, hears her. She kneels down, puts her arms around her, and says sympathetically, "Don't cry, Diana. I'll be your Mommy 'til your Mommy comes."

Commentary

The expression on Laurie's face reveals her distress over the crying. She is touching Diana with tenderness as she expresses her sympathy and understanding. She may remember how she felt when she was new at the center, and she appears to know that one can be comforted.

Young children have a capacity for feeling sympathy. Most young children are disturbed by a crying child. They may become uneasy because they fear what might happen to themselves, but if they are sufficiently secure, with a measure of trust in others, they are likely to try to relieve the unhappy child. Being able to comfort someone else is a positive act and makes the comforter feel good.

For a very young child, separation from the mother or family caregiver may feel like abandonment. It takes time for very young children to build a measure of trust that the parent or caregiver will return or be there when help is needed. The development of trust is one of the most important tasks of infancy and early childhood. Because trust is so important, separations from the familiar caregiver need to be planned with care.

When the separation is managed well, most children adjust comfortably because they enjoy being with other children. They are taking a step toward independence. We may wonder in this case whether the teacher has had enough time to build a relationship of trust with this unhappy child.

Feelings are strong when a child is young. The way these feelings are managed is likely to influence future relationships.

Questions to consider

How can parents and teachers insure that separation becomes a positive, rather than negative, experience? Consider varying kinds of separation, including those occasioned by divorce, incarceration, prolonged illness, and death.

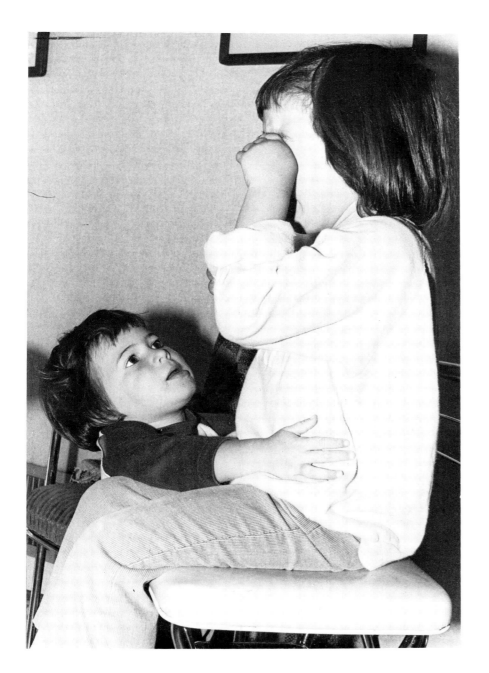

"You're not pretty"

Dolores and Monica are washing their hands before lunch. Eric is waiting his turn to wash. Out of the blue, he shouts crossly into Monica's face, "You're not pretty."

Into the stillness comes Dolores's firm voice, "Yes, she is. She looks just right for her."

Commentary

Dolores and Monica appear to enjoy washing their hands together in the same basin, but Eric is by himself, looking unhappy. When he blurts out, "You're not pretty," he directs the remark to the quieter, more vulnerable Monica. Dolores stands up for her friend, but she does not attack Eric. She just smiles and seems to want him to understand what her friend is like.

Dolores is certainly a friendly, comfortable child. She probably comes from a home where people are considerate and understanding. She feels secure and confident. She likes people and she expects to be liked. How we need such people in our world!

In contrast, Eric seems full of feelings of resentment. He is much less secure and confident. He gives the appearance that he does not expect to be liked. His feelings spill out in attacking remarks. Eric needs an adult to help him talk about his feelings. This will free him to discover that others are friendly and he can have fun with them. Helping this unhappy child gain confidence and more understanding of himself and others will take time and effort, but it will be worthwhile.

Feelings are important. Monica must feel reassured by the way her friend defended her. Eric may be surprised. People can live together comfortably, all kinds of people.

Questions to consider

What kinds of feelings do children express to others whom they perceive as being different? How do these feelings originate?

What are some positive ways to help children deal with anger?

How can we help children build self-confidence and good feelings about themselves?

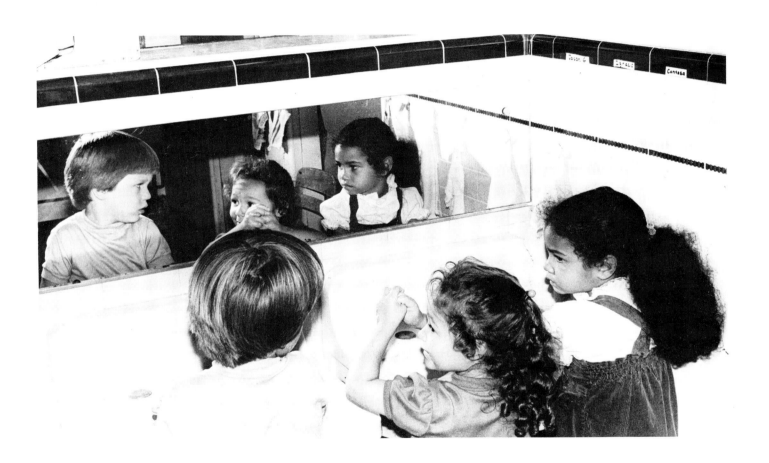

"We have company"

Jennie and Nancy love to play dress-up in the housekeeping corner. One morning they put their two babies in one buggy and walk toward the other end of the room. As they look back, Jennie, upset, cries out, "Look, look! The boys are getting into our house!"

Nancy turns around to see what is happening. Seeing the boys, she exclaims, "We have company. Let's go right back!"

Commentary

Intruders or friends? Does it depend on whom you are expecting?

Jennie seems to expect trouble. Her approach to the boys is likely to make them act like intruders, whether that was their intention or not. Nancy, in contrast, assumes that the boys are friends and hastens to return and welcome them. The two girls see the same situation quite differently.

In a sense, Jennie and Nancy tend to make the world into what they expect. Nancy expects to meet friends while Jennie expects difficulty. She may not trust others. It will take more observations to find whether the children's reactions in this situation are typical. Attitudes and patterns of behavior are established early. They probably arise from individual differences in ways of responding to circumstances and from the feelings of the adults who care for the child. But attitudes can change.

The task of the teacher, if Jennie consistently sees situations negatively, is to help Jennie discover a friendlier world. She needs to feel more confidence and trust in herself and her ability to cope with the world and the people in it. Playing with other children like Nancy will help her. The teacher can encourage Jennie to find avenues of creative expression for her negative feelings, such as drawing and painting. Negative feelings need to be drained off. As Jennie finds friends, her perception of the world may change. The teacher can also share her observations with Jennie's parents so they can work together to help Jennie. Attitudes of everyone can change.

Nancy has already discovered that being with people can be fun. Her world should prove to be interesting and satisfying.

Questions to consider

Think back to your own early childhood. Can you recall a particularly positive, or particularly negative, experience? Where did the experience occur? What did other people in the situation do? Did they help or hinder? Was the experience a typical one for you? How, if at all, do you think it may have influenced your social development?

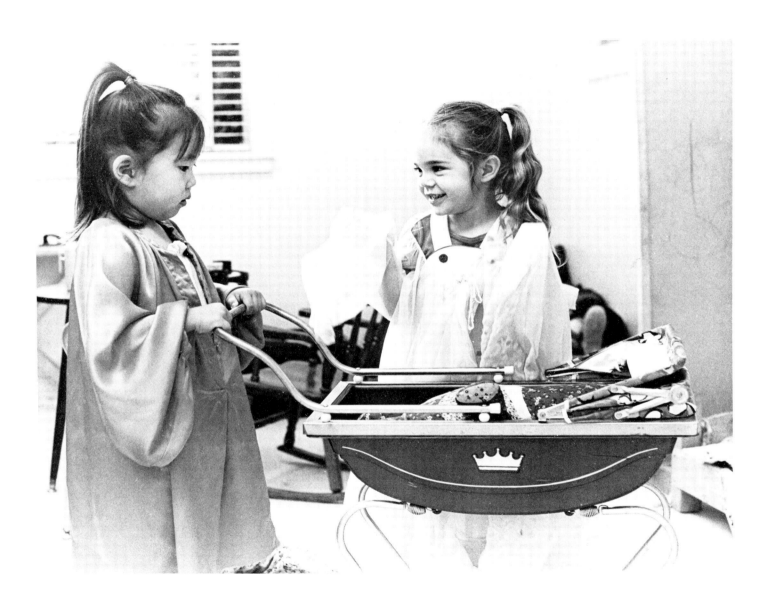

"Now go to work"

Jane and Amanda are playing in the housekeeping corner when David tries to join them. The girls don't want to play with him. He persists. They resist. Finally he turns to the teacher for help. The teacher responds by saying to the girls, "He wants to play with you so much. Maybe you can find something for him to do."

Amanda is very reluctant. Nevertheless, she decides, "OK, come on in," and lets David into their home. Immediately Amanda addresses David. "You're the daddy. Let me fix your tie. Here's your lunchbox. Now go to work. Goodbye." And she shoves him out of the housekeeping corner.

Commentary

Four-year-olds Jane and Amanda are resourceful children. They adjust well when the teacher intervenes for David. The two have been enjoying their play together and they manage to continue it by giving David the role of a daddy, a role which disposes of him in short order. In their lives, daddies and mommies often leave to go to work.

What is the result for David? He is still out in the cold. His problem still remains to be solved.

An understanding teacher, instead of appealing to the girls, might have asked David, "Do you think there may be something the girls would like to have you do?" If David is not equal to this challenge, the teacher may need to stimulate his thinking by suggesting, "What about being a carpenter or a grandfather?"

David may or may not have some success. If he does not, the teacher can state a fact, "The girls seem to want to play by themselves. People do sometimes." She might add, "Is there anyone else you might want to play with?" or "Have you painted any pictures lately?" or "I saw you building a high tower with the big blocks yesterday."

If David is a dependent child who lacks resourcefulness and social skills, his teacher will need to help him develop interests and gain confidence in himself. Teachers do need to facilitate children's social development when they are having difficulty. David has taken the first step by asking for help from his teacher. As he develops interests and skills, he will probably become a more acceptable playmate. David does need to go to work!

Questions to consider

How can teachers support children's social development?

Why is it important for children to acquire social skills?

And Listen to Parents When . . .

"What I wouldn't give for a job like yours"

Our early childhood program opens at 6 a.m. and closes at 6 p.m. One day, everything went wrong. A child tried to put a shoe down the toilet. The keys to the kitchen were lost. The milk was sour. The sprinklers went off while the children were playing on the lawn, and there weren't enough dry clothes for everyone. It was just a rotten day.

One mother called and said she would be late. The teacher who usually closed was ill, so another teacher had to stay. It had been a 12-hour day and she was tired. She held the child in her lap in a rocking chair to wait. When the mother finally arrived, she looked at the teacher and said, "Oh, what I wouldn't give for a job like yours where I could sit all day and rock."

Commentary

"If she only knew . . . " thinks a tired teacher as a feeling of resentment wells up at the parent's sarcastic remark. The teacher recalls all the day's frustrations, leading up to the final one when she had to stay late to care for a lonely child. She had been so glad to sink down into the Center's rocking chair with the child on her lap.

"If she only knew what my day has been like," thinks a tired parent as she glimpses the teacher relaxing in a rocking chair with *her* child contentedly looking at a picture book. It is just too much after a day when everything went wrong and she had to work overtime at the end. Her feelings just spill out in this thoughtless comment.

Of course the parent realizes that the teacher's job is a demanding one. She can imagine the problems facing anyone who is responsible for a group of young children. Of course, the teacher realizes the many problems that face a working mother. But both teacher and parent are human, and feelings may be hard to handle when there are so many frustrations in a day.

In spite of all their frustrations, parents and teachers do have a common concern—the welfare of the child. They need each other and the burdens are lighter when they respect one another.

Good relationships depend on communication: greetings in the morning, notes sent home by the teacher about significant happenings, conferences at convenient times, group meetings, even home visits.

When parent and teacher know and trust each other, the time may come when the parent is able to say, "You make me envious. I'm dead tired. I've had a terrible day." And the teacher may be able to reply, "You're really ready for a rest. Sit down for a few minutes and tell me about it. I've just had a day like that

myself." In this case, the parent, the teacher, and the child can benefit and grow. Early childhood education is about this kind of understanding.

Questions to consider

What kinds of experiences enable parents, teachers, and other staff members to trust one another?

What types of communication are most successful in developing a professional relationship with parents?

Acknowledgments

We wish to thank the California schools for allowing us to photograph their children, teachers, and volunteers . . .

Circle of Children, Santa Monica
Creative Center for Children, West Los Angeles
Edison Elementary School, Santa Monica
Home-SAFE Child Care Services, Los Angeles
John Adams Children's Center, Santa Monica
Lincoln Children's Center, Santa Monica
Mar Vista Family Center, Culver City
UCLA Child Care Services, West Los Angeles
UCLA Intervention School for Developmentally Handicapped Pre-school
    Children
and the Berlfein grandchildren, Sarah and Joey

and the additional storytellers . . .

Madeline Hunter, Harold Friedman, Dot Levens

and the reviewers . . .

Dorothy Hill and Kathe Jervis

51

Information About NAEYC

NAEYC is . . .

a membership-supported organization of people committed to fostering the growth and development of children from birth through age eight. Membership is open to all who share a desire to serve and act on behalf of the needs and rights of young children.

NAEYC provides . . .

educational services and resources to adults who work with and for children, including

- *Young Children,* the journal for early childhood educators
- **Books, posters, brochures,** and **videos** to expand your knowledge and commitment to young children, with topics including infants, curriculum, research, discipline, teacher education, and parent involvement
- An **Annual Conference** that brings people from all over the country to share their expertise and advocate on behalf of children and families
- **Week of the Young Child** celebrations sponsored by NAEYC Affiliate Groups across the nation to call public attention to the needs and rights of children and families
- **Insurance plans** for individuals and programs
- **Public affairs** information for knowledgeable advocacy efforts at all levels of government and through the media
- The **National Academy of Early Childhood Programs,** a voluntary accreditation system for high-quality programs for children
- The **National Institute for Early Childhood Professional Development,** providing resources and services to improve professional preparation and development of early childhood educators
- The **Information Service,** a centralized source of information sharing, distribution, and collaboration

For free information about membership, publications, or other NAEYC services . . .

- call NAEYC at 202-232-8777 or 800-424-2460
- or write to the National Association for the Education of Young Children, 1509 16th Street, N.W., Washington, DC 20036-1426.

About the Authors

JEAN REISS BERLFIEN, B.S., is a photographer in Los Angeles, California. Many of her photos have appeared in *Young Children* and other NAEYC publications, including *Mud, Sand, and Water*. She has produced several books and films in the field of child care and development, including NAEYC's filmstrip (now a video) *A Classroom With Blocks*.

MILLIE ALMY, Ph.D., is Professor Emerita at the University of California. She was President of NAEYC from 1952 to 1953 and is the author of many articles and books in the field. She has worked with young children as both a teacher and program director. On the university level, she has taught developmental psychology and early childhood education.

DOCIA ZAVITKOVSKY, M.S., is a child development consultant in California. NAEYC President from 1984 to 1986, former editor of *Young Children*'s predecessor, *The Journal of Nursery Education*, she is co-author of *Activities for School-Age Child Care*, published by NAEYC. She has worked with children as a teacher and program director.

KATHERINE READ BAKER, M.S., Professor Emerita, Oregon State University, was a teacher and director of programs for young children, taught courses in early childhood education, and conducted workshops for parents and teachers. She has contibuted articles to *Young Children*, wrote NAEYC's classic *Let's Play Outdoors*, and is author of *The Nursery School: Human Relationships and Learning*.

the stories . . .

out of the mouths of 3-, 4-, and 5-year-olds, some of whom may now be 45 years young.